LOVE YOUR FEAR

A QUICK SELF-HELP GUIDE
TO MANAGING ANXIETY

JOEL SCHUELER

Love Your Fear:

A Quick Self-Help Guide to Managing Anxiety

Copyright © 2019 by Joel Schueler

ISBN: 978-1-089176-04-6

London Oxford Press

Cover Design by Rick Holland

User note: The advice in this book is not intended to be used as a replacement for that of qualified behavioural or medical practitioners.

'I am an old man and have known a great many troubles,
but most of them never happened.'

Mark Twain

CONTENTS

INTRODUCTION

Dear Warrior,

Yes, you are not just a worrier but a warrior too, for you have taken the plunge to manage your fear. Note that I use the word *manage*, not *conquer*. The reason?

Fear will always be with us; accepting fear is the first step to managing it.

Firstly, it seems appropriate to define fear and anxiety so as to see more clearly how they differ. According to Catherine M Pittman and Elizabeth M Karle in *Rewire your Anxious Brain*, 'Anxiety is a complex emotional response that's similar to fear. Both arise from similar brain processes and cause similar psychological and behavioural reactions. Both originate in portions of the brain designed to help all animals deal with danger. Fear and anxiety differ however in that fear is typically associated with a clear present and identifiable threat whereas anxiety occurs in the absence of immediate peril. In other words, we feel fear when we actually are in trouble…we feel anxiety when we have a sense of dread or discomfort but aren't at that moment in danger.'

In another definition found at www.verywellmind .com: 'Fear relates to a known or understood threat, whereas anxiety follows from an unknown or poorly defined threat.'

The main title of this book is *Love your Fear*, but underneath that it says that the book is a guide to managing anxiety.

So which is it? Is this a book about fear or anxiety?

The answer is both. There are instances throughout this book where one of the terms is used but could just as easily be replaced for the other, or there are times where both may apply. This book encourages the rewording or rephrasing of its content by you, the reader, to match the words and phrases that fit best for you.

In *Rewire Your Anxious Brain*, Catherine M Pittman and Elizabeth M Karle tell us how in prehistory, high levels of anxiety were needed to survive. Anxiety helped to signal danger: 'We are the descendants of frightened people,' the authors declare. The authors go on to explain how the more casual cavepeople of this world would have been less likely to have survived because they would not have sensed danger as well as those that were more cautious.

To embrace fear means to embrace a part of you, a part of your history, and a part of what it means to be human. It goes some way to explaining your evolution. Take comfort from the strength of your genes and where they have taken you.

Fear is what we need to tells us a hungry lion is coming towards us. It sends a message from our brain to our body that we need to run like crazy and get the hell out of there. Yet fear can say *hello* at the most unlikely of locations and at the most unnecessary of times. When deep down we know we are perfectly safe, the fact that we can experience the same level of fear at home as when a hungry lion approaches us tells us that we cannot always find the answers to our anxiety through logic and reason. Fear does not need to be feared but can instead be seen as one of life's challenges to embrace. What happens to fear if we are able to remove our **sense** of self? If I am not fearful, where has fear got to?

Easier said than done, you might say, particularly as we anxious people can have more fear stored in our bodies than most. But if we are so highly attuned to our fears, then we are just as highly attuned to managing them.

Fear is like the unwelcome dinner guest. We do not want to be rude and tell it to go away. So what do we do with it? We accept fear is here as part of our life experience, knowing that as long as we are human it will not leave us because we need to know if the hungry lion is coming for us. Once we accept fear, we can discover and implement the methods to managing it.

Would you believe me if I told you there were lots of doubts I had in writing this book? I had many thoughts of self-doubt. I thought it would depress me to revisit difficult parts of my life that I would much rather forget. I was worried if anyone would be interested in this type of book. I was worried if anyone would read it. I was worried about all sorts of different things.

I still have fear but I have written this book. Once you have read this book and if you have read any other self-help books in a similar area, or have done exercises given to you by a psychologist or psychotherapist, you are still going to have fear in your life. There is no magic permanent cure. If you are under strong medication, then once you come off the medication you will still have fear in your life. So accept right now that you are going to still feel fear. However, this is not something to be worried about. Worrying about worry has surely got to be one of the silliest things us worriers do. But we all do it, and there are perfectly acceptable and understandable reasons for doing so.

Be confident about your fear. Be happy about your fear. Understand that the key to living with your fear is not to get rid of it or to try and cure it but to find the most practical and the most beneficial methods for your health to live with your fear. Love your fear.

I have tried to keep this book user-friendly and accessible, injecting pathetic attempts at humour where I can. I know what you might be thinking:

How is this book different to all the other books of a similar nature?

Well for one, I cut the crap. Reading other nonfictional self-help, I have become frustrated at how much of the reader's time is wasted. How many times and for how long do we need to hear about the author's rags to riches story, or how they have just gone on a magnificent holiday with their happy family and how you can live this lifestyle too, if only you were to follow the author's advice.

They may go on and on about their experiences and achievements or skirt around the heart of the matter, padding out their book with words for the sake of words, only revealing the good bits toward the end. Or maybe there is an overlong explanation of how you have to learn to do x, y and z for success, with one hundred examples of how to do x. y and z.

None of that here. There is no false hope. It would be my advice to see this book not as a source from which your life can radically improve. Rather, see this book as an aid to help you gather the tools—some of which may lie dormant within you or as yet be undiscovered—for managing your fear. Manage your fear and you might just love it.

Secondly, this book is written by someone with first-hand battles with fear, losing many of them, before I learned to love my fear, that is. My many different anxieties, though they may not directly correlate with yours, will no doubt at times have overlapped and continue to overlap with yours, for the anxious world is a broad spectrum.

There are touches on my own experiences with fear, and mechanisms that have helped me cope over nearly two decades with not only fear but also other, often related mental health problems. I am now in a stronger position to be able to write a book like this, doing what I love: my passion for writing. The stronger your position, the more **you** will be able to pursue your passions too.

Thirdly, whilst there is much to gain from useful information and structural considerations in other self-help books, *Love your Fear* does not adhere to a set formula of previous methods to inform its content. Instead, a study of such methods has been undertaken. With them in mind, ways have been thought of and developed so as to increase my ability to help a fellow mental health haver. Moreover, I have tried my best to help in a way that does not digress nor succumb to verbosity. So without further ado, let's get on with it.

CHAPTER 1

MIND OVER INSTINCT

'Acceptance and understanding
begin the process of bodily relaxation.'

Dr. Claire Weekes, *How to overcome Anxiety*

1.1 One Small Step

Fear is not that impressive. I can think of far greater enemies. In fact, with time and effort, we can manage it by taking small steps in the right direction. There arises a time in all our lives when there are so many different tasks to do. The tasks have accumulated to a seemingly insurmountable list, and it seems like there will never be enough time to do them all. You are left stressed, depressed and overwhelmed. At this point it is easy to freeze. The key to being free is simpler than it seems. Doing one task at a time makes for a good start.

One little task is all it takes to set you on your way. You can pick any task, however small, that is on your list of things to do, and, if you can, try and do the tasks in priority of importance. Some people might like to get more into the detail of how they arrange this sense of priority. For me, it was a case of thinking but not overthinking about what seemed the most pressing task, rather than making an actual list of tasks to do. Some may think more pictorially and want a list or a diagram of their tasks laid out in front of them.

In any case, a method that has often proven fruitful for me is not only doing the most pressing task but also that which seems the most tedious or difficult, first. The effort needed will be greater in order to complete the most tedious or difficult task but so will the sense of achievement afterwards, and every task thereafter will seem easier.

You will feel your confidence start to grow, even if you choose the easiest or quickest task first. If you are not sure which way round to order your tasks, then experiment, empowering yourself by finding within the method that works best for you.

Doing builds confidence. Always remember this. Try and get into a habit of **not** saying, *O God, I can't do that. I haven't the time. I haven't the energy.*

Do what you can bit by bit. One small step at a time. It might not seem like much, but it **will** help. It might help to use the following method in the next subchapter.

1.2 The Doing Method

Part 1: Do One Task

Part 2: Do The Next Task(s)

Part 3: Confidence Grows

Parts 1 & 2 = The 'Doing' Parts. Part 3 = The End Result.

In my experience, when it comes to mental health problems, the way you experience the world can be completely different one hour to the next, let alone one day to the next. Perhaps you can relate.

The funny thing I have found is that I can have a majorly productive or confidence-building day one day, and then the next I can wake up and feel like all my hard work has been in vain and I am back to square one or worse. I feel at that moment that it is going to take a monumental effort to get anywhere near to making the new day productive.

But then…the method…do one task, and however hard it might feel to progress, you are back on the cycle—perhaps it will feel like a unicycle at first, but you will know that it could feel like a motorcycle soon again.

1.3 Letting Go

It is our inbuilt nature to resist and defend when a problem creeps up. In the majority of cases it is best to override such an instinct. A way we can do this is by *letting go*. You may have heard of this term in relation to meditation or mindfulness. If you are not exactly sure what meditation or mindfulness is, the good news is that you don't need to be. If you are in this boat then it is a very large boat and there's plenty room for one more, so hop on board, and for now think of meditation as something you do sitting down with your eyes closed, and mindfulness as something you can do at any moment as you live day to day. Think of both meditation and mindfulness as meaning *awareness*.

I can hear some of those advanced in meditation and mindfulness recoil and say:

What are you talking about?

But hold your horses, I am helping out the newbies, or as I am led to believe as they are referred to in the gaming community, *noobs.*

Meditation or Mindfulness?

It is best to use a combination of the two. Mindfulness will help us throughout the day and increase our powers of concentration in the long run. When we find a quiet moment where we will not be disturbed, meditation will allow us to go deeper in the practice.

Know that although letting go is an important meditative instruction, it is also far from being the only one, and it can be problematic to use letting go as our 'go-to' for a peaceful mind. Furthermore, it can be problematic to try and let go too quickly. Letting go can be a powerful technique, but what exactly does it mean and how do we do it?

If you have, for example, a bad foot, and that is the most pressing thing on your mind, then use that as what we will call *the most pressing subject of awareness.* You can do this sitting down and closing your eyes or during a free moment in your everyday life. Right now don't close your eyes as you won't be able to follow the instructions. Pause for some seconds before each sentence as we do this, going at a pace to suit you. Substitute the bad foot for the most pressing subject of awareness. It may be a pain, a sound, a thought, an emotion, what you will. Watch this most pressing subject of awareness as a nonjudgmental observer.

Just watch, no judgment. How does this thing change? Does it become more pressing or less?

Congratulations! You have just completed the meditative exercise. The most advanced meditators can easily forget the simple power of just observing. Just to watch. That is all. It is very easy to get caught up in so many different techniques learnt over the years when it comes to meditation and mindfulness. But keep it simple. This point cannot be emphasised enough.

People often come to meditation or mindfulness to deal with something difficult in their lives. Therefore, this difficult something is often their most pressing subject of awareness. Whether it is physical pain, emotional pain, or some other difficulty, the natural desire is to want to eradicate it. Unfortunately, this desire cannot always be fulfilled. But we can improve our situation by letting go of what is difficult.

But how do you let go of a pain?

Ask my ex-wife for more info. Letting go means letting go of our attachment or of our 'clinging' to the pain. The meditation teacher, Gil Fronsdal, once said, 'If you cling you will suffer—money back guaranteed.'

We may not be able to let go of the pain in its inherent constitution, but we **can** let go of our attitude towards it, and we **can** let go of our attachment to it a.k.a. how we cling to it. This is a key point. If you have in any small way explored the mind and how you can use it positively then this is magnificent news. Never underestimate the power of your mind.

John Cleese was once talking about a General in the British Army who said something that struck him.

All the General said was, 'Very little matters much, and most things don't matter at all.'

It struck me too, as it is simple yet holds much truth. Let us think for a moment. Let us think broadly of all the things we have worried about up until now. How many of them have really mattered all that much at all? Probably very few of them. As many people get older, rather than becoming sadder they become happier because an awful lot of the things that they worried about when they were younger they realise now never actually mattered very much.

Looks can fade, health can deteriorate, and yet happiness can bloom. Perchance there is less to cling on to as we olden. If we are young, healthy and mobile, it can feel like we have the world at our feet. How easy it is to cling onto what we do not want to let go of. How much easier is it when we let go of the things that do not really matter? At the very least, we experience a tranquillity and find some beauty in acceptance. At our core, it is important to have what Dr. John P. Forsyth—probably unrelated to Bruce—talked about in an interview on *Inspire Nation Show*: 'A willingness to let go of what is not working.'

It can be too easy to think of letting go as something we say or think to ourselves, but afterwards it may feel like nothing happens. It is easy then to feel frustrated or bored with the whole process, and our mind starts wandering to what we will have for dinner tonight. At this juncture, I feel it is important to repeat that it can be problematic to use letting go as our 'go-to' for a peaceful mind, and that it can also be problematic to try and let go too quickly. It is especially true that when we have a really difficult pressing subject of awareness, it is natural that we are desperate to let go of it. But if we try and let go of something too quickly, it might not work, and we can lose faith in the idea of trying to let go of it when it does not seem to want to budge. To know when to 'stay' with something or to let go of something a skill we develop, often through trial and error. Improving the efficacy of our decision-making, this is where wisdom plays its hand.

Sometimes it is best to observe the pain for longer even if we really want to let go of it, and, using wisdom, we determine when it is best to let go of it. An example of wisdom developing through trial and error: we have a pain we try to let go of very quickly. It does not work, so we try to focus on letting go some more, and we can feel our frustration and anger start to increase. We say to ourselves, *ok this isn't working, let me try and observe it for longer.* We observe it for longer and can feel a slight alleviation of the pain, or the pain has moved or changed slightly. We observe how the pain manifests now but do not seem to be making much headway. Maybe it is best to try and let go again, this time having a positive result in that it is that little bit easier to let go of the pain this time, and we feel more at peace.

It is easy to think of pain as something fixed, and it can often feel that way. But if we watch it for long enough, it is amazing how often we can see it change. And I use the word *amazing* because I would like to encourage you to be open to amazing results. Have a childlike sense of wonder and direct it at pain: looking at the pain like we have never seen it before, as if it is the most incredible entity.

When we meditate or are mindful, we are not 'doing' anything. We are returning to our primordial nature. If you have a child in a room with other adults, then observe that child. They are likely to be the most mindful person in the room. Why? Because generally their wonder is greater, being 'in the moment' more than adults, who are often thinking about thousands of things like their energy bill or how much they dislike their boss. That is why children can be happy at the littlest happening. We have forgotten our childlike sense of wonder.

1.4 Relating to Mind

Thinking is not the enemy; the way we relate to it is. The mind is not our enemy; its hold on us is. These things in themselves are as they are, and it is important for us even if we are not able or ready to change our relationship with them, to be aware of what is going on. When our minds are in control of us, we are at their mercy. Back and forth, to and fro, wherever the mind wants to go, we follow like sheep. The mind says, *I want chocolate. I want that bike. I want this, I want that*, and off we go thinking that fulfilling our desires will give us happiness. But once we acquire that object of desire, we simply look to the next one. It is ongoing, we are back in another cycle: a cycle of never quite being satisfied. If we relate this to our anxious thoughts and desires—*if only I was less anxious, when will I stop this silly worrying? I wish I could just relax and enjoy life*— how often do these thoughts actually help us?

You can live your life relating to mind in this cyclic way relatively happily because if you have enough money you can keep getting that next object of desire and the short-term desires mould into a quenching of long-term desires. With this model, it will be tricky to find deep happiness because you will always be a slave to your mind, in a similar way to being addicted to a drug.

When your mind controls you, you are its slave. When **you** control your mind, your life becomes something quite extraordinary, that others around can feel—a blessing for you and everyone else around you.

In Robert Satterfield's book, *Anxiety*, there is the suggestion to set up a designated worry period where you can worry as much as you want. As soon as the designated worry period is over, you are not allowed to worry anymore.

This method reminds me of intermittent fasting. An intermittent fasting for the mind. Personally, I have not tried this method but if you feel it might be something that could benefit you then why not give it a go.

Once I heard a meditation teacher talk about the mind being like a bird. Most of the time the bird is flying around like crazy and then when you put it in the cage, it is contained. Now although I can understand what he is saying, this analogy does not quite work for me because I quite like the idea of the bird being free rather than in a cage, but you can see the idea he is getting at: When you have more control over your mind, you have more freedom.

In addition, when you have more control over your mind, you have more control over your fear. What are some of the unhelpful ways you relate to mind? An awareness of these unhelpful ideas and thoughts is a huge first step to having more control over them. It then becomes easier to let go of them, or defeat them in battle if you wish to take that approach.

Think about more beneficial thoughts, desires and goals you can apply to your life. Test them out and ask yourself: *Are these new thoughts, desires and goals actually helping me?* If not, find others that will.

On the mind, Dr. John P. Forsyth says, 'We think of *it* (the mind) as us and we take our thoughts so literally and so seriously, so the perspective-taking is we step back from our thoughts. The next critical question is really to ask ourselves—here's my mind, my old history feeding me this news—is this thought helpful to me in the service of me doing what matters, (of) me living the life that I want to lead?'

1.5 Finding the Time

There was a story about a meditation teacher and a student. The student was a busy mum who said she wanted to meditate but was simply too busy to find the time to sit down and meditate quietly. The teacher did not believe her at first so he went to go and live with her for several days to see if it was true. By the end of his time there, he agreed with her. She really did not have the time. So his instruction to her was—whenever she walked across the hall of her home from room to room in-between attending to the children—to use that hall as her meditation space.

The student's concentration got better and better, being mindful at each step she took across the hall. Over time, her concentration became strong.

Some months later when she had the time to go on a meditation retreat, she was able to quickly get into a deep meditational state thanks to all the training she had done.

Bear this in mind as an example, that however busy you are, there is always a way to find time for meditation or mindfulness.

1.6 A Note on Breathing

A focus on breathing helps us in times of stress and also during meditation and mindfulness. Robert Satterfield says that, 'Breathing also helps the body go from a fight or flight response of the sympathetic nervous system (SNS) to the relaxed response of the parasympathetic nervous system (PSNS)…It is very crucial to breathe through your nose since breathing through the nose stimulates nerve cells that exist behind the sternum near the spine that trigger the parasympathetic nervous system. Anxiety is a sympathetic response and parasympathetic counteracts that. This calms your body which then slowly calms your mind.'

CHAPTER 2

CONFIDENCE IN GUT INSTINCTS

In considering the previous chapter, we should also not dismiss our gut instincts, what they can teach us, and why we do not have to be afraid in developing confidence in them.

2.1 Help from Others

I have been treated by different counsellors and psychotherapists, some of them good, some not so good. Despite their professional training, a problem I have seen arise and re-arise is that they may not have actually lived my experience or yours, applicable to the problems we present them. Therefore, there can be a problem in understanding where we are truly coming from, even if they mean well and are the most brilliant scholars on the subject. Life experience of a problem is a great gateway for its understanding.

For example, let us first consider depression. You may have the most excellent psychotherapist who happens to have had personal experience with mental health problems in their life, but none of those specifically have been depression, at least not a serious bout of depression or not by any chronic stretch, and not so bad that they cannot get out of bed or have had trouble going to work or have been crying every day. But they are treating **you**, specifically for **depression**. So it is no fault of their own, but it is just a fact that we are often treated by someone who does not have the same experience as us, with methods more likely formulaic than bespoke.

This is where I have found some problems in my own treatment. The practitioner will get some worksheets or printed handouts for you and they will say things like: *one of the best things you can do is do some exercise for your problems*, or they will tell you statistics from a text book. *You might want to join the gym or do some yoga or play a sport etcetera.*

Of course, the practitioner is right. These are excellent tools for mental health but they might not be the right things for you to be doing at this particular moment in time. You may feel unready to do any of these kind of activities because at the moment all you are focussed on is getting out of bed every day. I have had instances where I have felt terrible after exercise and as a result have felt tired and frustrated at such a waste of time because I am spent for the rest of the day or evening when I could have been productive had I not done that exercise.

The worksheets possibly take the form of daily planners of what you need to do and how you like to organise your weeks, but for some individuals this is not very helpful. It certainly wasn't for me. I never found anything from those daily planner sheets—that is not how I organise the thoughts in my head to do what I need to do on a daily basis. For some people they might work and they like to have that sense of planning and that daily picture in their head. So, great if that works. I found a lot of methods generic, and from of a system that tells the psychotherapists what they should relay to us to help us. The methods are recycled for all their clients. They are not tailored to the client's personality unless you kick up a fuss at which point you can feel like you are the one being unfair and battling with someone trying to help you on top of your own personal battles already, or you might not feel confident enough to challenge these specialists of authority in their field.

Nice rant, Schueler, but what has all this got to do with loving your fear and/or being confident in gut instincts?

The reason I am mentioning all this is that if you are relatively new to a mental health problem that you are struggling with then do not dismiss your confidence in your gut instincts in what feels the best method for you in managing it. That is not to say you should dismiss professional advice, far from it. But create strong ideas of what you think will and will not work for you as you receive advice and research possibilities. Even if your confidence feels like a little mouse in the corner at the moment, do not dismiss **your confidence** however small in what you feel when you are asked to do a particular task like a daily planner sheet as a case in point. If something does not feel right for you, and that is your gut instinct at the time when you are first told about the task, then that is probably not going to change.

Though the practitioner may keep asking you to do something a number of times, the longer you leave telling them it is not working for you, the harder you might find it to tell them. If you are not sure about a task, then by all means try it if you have not tried it before, but if you are still not sold on it after doing it then that will help you to tell the therapist.

Love your confidence. Love that you have a strong sense in what you believe will work for you. It may seem hard or not come naturally to you but you are being kind to yourself by making a stand.

If you can find the confidence but not the words, then you can use the following template when you disagree with the practitioner: *No I am sorry but that is not going to work for me. I know it is what I have been asked to do for my benefit to try and help me. I know that you trying to help but I really feel that is not the right method for me. Can we please try* something else *that might work better for me?*

If the practitioner is not willing to do that or keeps insisting that you do it, then it might be an idea to find someone that has a different approach and who can work better with you, and/or you can find what other information and approaches feel more appropriate to you in your own spare time. Yes, experience is valuable, and you can learn a lot from trial and error, but even at the early stages with a practitioner or in other unsure moments in your life, have confidence in your gut instincts. Even if you and your gut instincts change course, at the very least be aware of them and take note of them.

Gut instincts are powerful. They are not always right, but more times than not they are. That is my experience anyhow. They are like our subconscious friends, telling us something before we even know it.

Think now about your gut instincts in the past. Have they usually been right more often than not? In any case, what have you learned from them? If they seem to be or have been wrong more times than right, they are still a communication to us, and to ignore them is to do ourselves a disservice.

If you are thinking about soliciting the services of a therapist, then it is important to find the right therapist for you. Think about whether it would make a difference to you regarding the gender of the therapist. If you are dealing with sensitive issues attributable to your gender, then you might find it more comfortable to choose a therapist who identifies in the same way as you do. Other things to think about are: do they have a good website? Have they shown that they have taken care on their website?

My feeling always is that if they have not properly bothered to create a good professional-looking website or put a good profile on a therapist directory page, then this worries me, particularly if I am looking for someone to help me worry less. It worries me that they might not have as much care for their profession or clients as they should. See if they have similar interests to you, and whether they treat or even specialise in the area of help you are looking for. Sometimes they will the state their interests and the kind of customised service they provide. I found that I had a good experience with a therapist who was of an alternative and spiritual persuasion that aligned well with my personality and interests. She turned out to be one of the best counsellors I had.

I am based in the UK and that is where my experiences have been formed. However, there may be similarities to your experiences if you are in another country too. When it comes to counselling, there are now better services for getting counsellors on the National Health Service (NHS) than I remember ten or fifteen years ago. But there are usually waiting times and sometimes these can be quite long, and you may require something quicker if you are in a particularly difficult situation and seek treatment as soon as possible. If you are able to go down the private route, makc sure you are getting your money's worth and try not to be afraid to change the therapist if you feel they are not right for you. Like my mum says, you get what you pay for.

It can help to talk with others who are going through similar experiences to you. There may be online forums or Facebook groups or local social events like on www.meetup.com where you can meet like-minded people to share experiences and support each other. I have written a list of charities and organisations at the end of this book that you might find of use too.

CHAPTER 3

TYPES OF ANXIETY DISORDERS

According to MG Craske and MB Stein in *The Lancet*: about 12% of adults are affected by an anxiety disorder in a given year. (Source: www.bbrfoundation-.org) This figure is 18% in the USA.

In *OCD & Anxiety Disorders: Crash Course Psychology #29*, it is said that, 'Anxiety disorders are characterised not only by distressing, persistent anxiety but also often by the dysfunctional behaviours that reduce that anxiety,' and 'At least a fifth of all people will experience a diagnosable anxiety disorder...at some point in their lives.'

Anxiety is the most common mental health problem. It is estimated that as many as forty million Americans alone currently have an anxiety disorder.

We see in the behaviour of cats that the more they are stared at, the more they can feel on edge, and their ears go back as they watch your every move, particularly if they are not familiar with you and/or are one of the more anxious cats out there. In *Rewire Your Anxious Brain*, it is mentioned how lots of people staring at you is likely to trigger an anciently inbuilt anxious response. For instance, in the time of cavepeople, being stared at by lots of people might have meant you were another tribe's dinner. At the least it could represent a threat.

These examples help explain social anxiety, and also why the fear of public speaking is so common. Both are scientifically totally understandable. An important point and irony to remember is that everyone is too busy worrying about themselves to worry about your worry.

There are numerous anxiety disorders and some of the most common are: Social Anxiety Disorder, Post-Traumatic Stress Disorder (PTSD), Obsessive Compulsive Disorder (OCD), Seasonal Affective Disorder (SAD) - (Note that the acronym, *SAD* is also sometimes used for Social Anxiety Disorder), Panic Disorder, Generalised Anxiety Disorder, and phobias.

I have first-hand experience of PTSD. According to www.bbrfoundation.org, in PTSD, 'Very intense fearful experiences, especially those that are life threatening, are often "over-learned" and can lead to an unhealthy level of anxiety.'

I remember a previous psychotherapist describing the mind processing the traumatic event as like a broken record. You go into survival mode which allows you to remain relatively calm and get through the extreme situation. The only problem with this is that afterwards you have not processed the event properly and hence the flashbacks and the pain are still stored inside you.

Eye movement desensitization and reprocessing (EMDR) treatment, as well as the antidepressant, sertraline, were the two treatments that helped me the most.

In the UK, EMDR is very difficult to get on the NHS and if you are able to get it, you may be restricted to the number of sessions you can have. Unfortunately, people who suffer PTSD often need help quickly and it is usually quicker to get private treatment. If you are in a position where you can pay for treatment, then I feel it is important to reiterate the need to try and get your money's worth and be assertive with your therapist and what you want from the sessions. It is easy for EMDR to not feature as often as you would like it to in sessions, and so try to find the confidence to be assertive in what you want.

Meditation and mindfulness have also been very helpful to me.

My general anxiety has improved a little by gradual exposure. This means making yourself encounter situations you find difficult one step at a time. You might try and force yourself into more difficult situations the more your confidence grows, but there is no need to overdo it, and you can start off on something that feels quite easy: this could be joining a class or going to a social event for example.

3.1 Relating to Worry

As Robert Satterfield talks of in *Anxiety*, we can put our worries into two categories: 'unjustified worries' and 'justified worries.' If you are not sure which of the two categories a worry fits into, ask yourself these two questions:

Is the worry realistic? Do you actually really believe this worry?

If you answer to either of these questions is *yes*, then it is a justified worry, but if the answer is *no*, it is unjustified. If you have a selection of different worries racing around your head, try and fit these into the two categories. Divide a page in half and have *Justified Worries* at the top of the first half of the page and *Unjustified Worries* at the top of the second. Maybe you could write down the main ones that crop up for you during the week. You will notice in future weeks you might have the same or very similar worries. Seeing the unjustified worries more than once confirms for you just how unjustified they are as you have called them out as being unjustified more than once. It may be helpful to reword the sections based on your preferences. The writer, Amber Rae divides worries into the two sections: 'toxic worry' and 'useful worry.' Satterfield also later explains in *Anxiety* how you can divide problems into 'solvable' and 'unsolvable problems.' You brainstorm the solvable problems such as how you can avoid being late for work by going to bed earlier the previous night or setting an alarm and so on.

Have joy in the fact that you do not need to hang on to the unsolvable problems any longer.

CHAPTER 4

CONSCIOUSNESS

(Source: www.thecoachingtoolscompany.com)

'The fear of annihilation, of ceasing to exist. This is more than just a "fear of death" or how we might die - it strikes at the very heart of our fear that we would simply no longer BE.'

Dr. Karl Albrecht

I think every human being would be lying if they said they were not at least a bit scared with regards to the above quote. What worries me the most personally is sudden unexpected death: The idea that we can be going along dandily and then the next minute everything we have ever known is gone without warning and we are without time to spend our final hours with our loved ones. If I know in advance that I am likely to die soon, then as awful as that still would be, I would take a little comfort from the fact that I had the time to mentally prepare for it and tell those that needed to know, spending the precious hours I have left with them.

Many of you with problems with fear may have looked into relaxation techniques and then by doing so have stumbled upon spiritual instructions that link in with this such as meditation and mindfulness and deep breathing techniques. That was how I first came to develop my spirituality by listening to podcasts such as 'Audio Dharma' and 'Zencast' for instructions about how to meditate, and I found the teacher that most struck a chord with me was Gil Fronsdal.

Spirituality does not have to have religious connotations, nor does it have to involve a deity. It affords a platform to join the dots together of what is beyond the science we know. It is about having an open mind to what is but what we cannot see. There are themes that run though ancient spiritual peoples, mystics and Sadhus of numerous generations. Connections can be found in what they say and what people who have near death experiences say. Reincarnation is often seen by such people as fact not opinion.

I personally am irreligious but I am open-minded as to that which we cannot explain and how this marries the science we have gathered. There is also the common theme I hear from many different spiritual people that our human body is merely a vehicle through which we experience life and that when this body is taken from us, our consciousness lives on. This has given me more confidence about dying. I would hate to believe in something for the sake of comfort. I am not saying that I believe in reincarnation, and I have listened to very convincing arguments by the likes of Christopher Hitchens, Richard Dawkins and Lawrence Krauss, and to a very large degree I find myself agreeing with what they say.

However, there is to an extent a trust that I have established as to the authenticity of the connected spiritual messages and spiritual nature of people's near death experiences. Just maybe, there is truth in reincarnation, non-duality, karma and other spiritual phenomena. It is easy when we are vulnerable to believe in the next magical message that is going to make our life better, or in the next spiritual teacher, or in the next religion we discover. We must always be able to question everything and never be convinced by someone else if we are not sure in our own minds. It is surely our human duty. Indeed, please question what I write here too. Question that last sentence and this one.

I believe that these voices from the spiritual world should be heard even if not on the same wavelength as our own. I believe it is right to not give in to comfort except perhaps in extreme distress, but I believe that whilst I have my doubts, that there is no harm in believing that such a vast networked history of these voices and those of near death experiences might just begin to cross the borders of truth of what we cannot see. They give hope, and hope is a great driver in humankind. It spurs us on to, at the minimum, reduce worry and make the most of this life we can see.

CHAPTER 5

WHAT WE TELL OURSELVES

5.1 Word Usage & Affirmations

As Eckhart Tolle says in *The Power of Now,* use words in preference of others that hold less meaning for you. For example, whenever I tried to tell myself, *relax,* it somehow just did not resonate with me in the same way as if I said the word, *calm.*

So to get in the state I desired, I started using the word *calm* instead of *relax.* I think *don't worry* has got to be one of the worst things you can say to an anxious person, but perhaps you will disagree.

Susan Jeffers, in her book, *Feel the Fear and Do It Anyway*, endorses the use of positive affirmations. You might find this ties in too much with the ego and is therefore unhelpful, but once again, find for you what works best. Affirmations she suggested that stand out for me, and that I may have altered slightly to suit me are, 'I'm powerful loved and loving,' and, in the true spirit of loving your fear, 'Everything is happening perfectly,' and 'I will feel anxiety as long as I continue to grow.' *Grow* in this context means growing and developing as a person. That is to say character-building through life. What positive affirmations can you think of that you could apply to your life?

Dr. John P. Forsyth says that we can choose to see 'Pain instead of as the enemy, (as) a teacher…maybe inside the feeling of anxiety there's a message that tells you that you care enough to feel strongly about something.'

What kind of affirmations can you make out of this quote? Can you flip over some of your other negative, unhelpful thoughts to give them a positive slant? You could try making some new affirmations out of those too.

5.2 How we think of Thoughts

Gil Fronsdal says that we are our own worst story-tellers. Mark Twain's quote at the start of this book is a great example of that. How often do our thoughts tell us a story of terrible events that will befall in the future? How many of them actually come true? If we documented all of our worried thoughts in a day of what might happen in the future, the ratio of these events not happening in actuality would no doubt vastly outweigh them. Why do we give so much power to our thoughts? Why, when they are so often false?

These predictions of future events of impending gloom are simply thoughts. It is amazing how much power we can give our thoughts. Just thoughts. They hold no power unless we give them power. If someone says something to us that hurts us, that breaches our insecurities, we might feel that criticism more because it has touched us emotionally in a negative way and we might start to believe it more. But why do we give these comments other people say to us so much power? If we are wrong with so many of our thoughts, what is to say other people aren't too? Why do we let these people play on our fears? If there are falsities with our thoughts and there are falsities with other people's thoughts, then there must be a falsity with fear itself.

'There is a battle of two wolves inside us all. One is evil. It is anger, jealousy, greed, resentment, lies, inferiority and ego. The other is good. It is joy, peace, love, hope, humility, kindness, empathy and truth. The wolf that wins? The one you feed.'

Cherokee Proverb

The above is a much-used quote but I have repeated it for the benefit of those who have not heard it before because it suitably connects with this subchapter.

5.3 Positivism & Balance

Some people say, *be positive*, or try to add as many positive influences to their lives. In a way, I think that is great. If they are able to do that all the time, then it is certainly better than being negative all the time. However, for some people, myself included, I do not think that could work. I do not have the energy or feel well enough often enough to be positive all the time, or to attempt to be positive as much as possible. It would be too draining. What comes up tends to come down, and therefore if you are positive and then have a bad time of it, then maybe you can crash harder. For me, positivism is great but I think within balance can be found a more realistic long-term happiness. I agree with the Buddhists on this. They call it finding the 'Middle Way.' It means not getting too high when things go well and not getting too low when things go badly.

You will notice this too with meditation. Gil Fronsdal says meditation is a lubricator in your life. It makes the day go a bit smoother. You are not so quick to snap at others or situations that do not go your way because it is like you feel you have more time between what takes place in life and your reactions to them. As well as time, it feels like you have more space to manoeuvre how you would like to in life rather than being pulled there by instinct. It is not that you become this different person who is more chilled out more often, it is that more stress falls away, allowing you to become more of the person you really are. This is certainly the case if we are able to get to a stage where we are meditating every day, even if only for ten minutes. We can really notice it if we are meditating every day and then one day we stop meditating. We can really notice the difference in how we are. We may not notice much on the days that we do meditate but we can really notice it on the day that we stop, as things may well feel more unsmooth and a bit more stressful. I think the old saying, *You don't know what you've got 'til it's gone*, holds true here.

If what we crave is the wealth to sunbathe on a paradisaical island and then, as Gil Fronsdal says, a crab comes and pinches us on the toe, suddenly we are not in paradise anymore. Therefore, it is unwise to rely too heavily on reaching the highs of the external world. Our inner world is where we can find deep lasting peace and happiness.

CHAPTER 6

SELFLESS OVER SELFISH

There is an old Buddhist parable that demonstrates the importance of self-care. There are two trapeze artists without a safety net about to perform a death-defying stunt. They have to grab hold of each other mid-air at the right time or they will fall to their death. One trapeze artist says to the other, 'I'm going to look out for you. I'm going to focus my attention on saving you.'

The other trapeze artist says, 'No. I will look after what I am doing, and you look after what you are doing. That way we will be helping each other.'

Why they decide to talk about all this just before they are to jump, I am not sure, and to my mind represents bad planning. But the message of the parable is that: **You have got to help yourself so that you can help others**. It is a similar message on aeroplanes where in an emergency, one is advised to put on an oxygen mask before helping someone else, or the popular saying that says we need to love ourselves first before we can expect anyone else to love us.

There is nothing selfish about this, nor is there in going away to meditate in a quiet place. They are acts of care for ourselves, and we are of far less help to others if we are stressed out and anxious.

So a primary act of care for ourselves is actually selfless rather than selfish because one of the main reasons we do it is so that we can be in a better position to help others.

6.1 Love without Conditions; Love without Attachment

It is often said that a mother's love for her child is unconditional. What a great place to start for a child coming into this world. Many people who are spiritually minded try and expand this to loving everyone, not just unconditionally but also without attachment. It is impossible to expect to be able to do this right away with success, so it is something developed over time and a good easy place to start this expansion is with others that are close to like friends and other family members because we tend to find them more tolerable than all the other lovely people we have to deal with. Can you imagine what kind of a world it would be if everyone could do this? Wishful thinking perhaps, but that it is possible gives hope for the betterment of the human condition.

But what has this got to do with my anxiety?

When we romantically long for a person we cannot have, this is an example of deep attachment. How many tears have we cried? How much sadness has been created because of these thoughts? Most specifically, how much anxiety has this caused us?

If we counted up the minutes we had spent with such thoughts and added them to the time spent with the negative ways they make us feel, we would realise that we have spent days, weeks, months, maybe years of our lives spent with this negativity.

If we are able to not attach, then if we love someone who does not love us, we can still be happy. We can still love them and be happy for them if they find someone else.

Of course we are talking about things that are very easy to say but extremely hard to do. It is more of a goal to work towards. Although loving unconditionally is usually easier to do with people close to you, you may find that letting go of attachment is easier in relation to people you love less.

Do not get too bogged down with the bigger picture or the fact that it seems too hard a job to accomplish. Just by making a start, you can reduce your anxiety as well as all the other negative thoughts and emotions often conflated with attachment. Now there is less anxiety to love. Now there is less fear to love.

CHAPTER 7

MORE MEDITATIONS

A simple way of viewing meditation and mindfulness is: stop and look. We are taking time out from our busy minds in a busy world to take a look at what is. To see the true nature of our consciousness in the midst of all the external images we see with our eyes. How often our eyes lie to us! Below are two more simple meditations anyone can do.

7.1 Simple Breath Meditation

With your back arched slightly, sit up straight, alert yet relaxed. An alert relaxedness. Eyes half-closed. Quiet your thoughts. Do three deep breaths to start. Then breathe normally. As you breathe normally, concentrate as many milliseconds as you can on the now. How much can you concentrate attentively without trying too hard—alert yet relaxed. How does it feel if you watch so carefully the breath in and out? If something more pressing comes into your awareness, you can turn your attention to that, but have in mind a gentle motivation to keep returning to the breath. Each time you lose focus and enter the world of thinking, do not become annoyed with yourself. Simply return to the breath with a light motivation to stay there. Continue until you reach what feels a natural conclusion.

7.2 Ten Minute Meditation & Afterthoughts

Once again, sitting comfortably, alert yet relaxed, eyes half-closed, give yourself permission to leave behind every single problem and worry on your mind, just for these ten minutes. Promise yourself that for these ten minutes you are going to try and let go of everything. It is OK, nothing is going to run away. After ten minutes you can come back to all your worries if you want. You don't need to worry about forgetting them. Just leave them for ten minutes. (In fact, you might even remember them better or think of other worries that relate to these worries when you come back to them, for your mind will be fresher.) You do not need to concentrate on the fact that you are breathing or think *how long should I breathe out for*? Am *I breathing out the right way?*

Whilst concentrating on the breath, or if you prefer, on the most pressing subject of awareness, be aware of the nature of your concentration.

Freedom comes from concentration. Can you concentrate in a way that does not feel like you are trying?

Have confidence that some of the answers to your life will be helped by the meditation because afterwards you will feel fresher and renewed just like you would after a nap. Give yourself permission to fall in the present moment. Dive in. As Eckhart Tolle says, there is no ego in the now. Loss of ego = loss of worry. Know presence. Just know it. Know it without judging it.

Knowledge is power and this kind of knowledge is self-power. With it we can eventually remove the self, or rather our sense of self and all the conceptual ideas we have created around it which hinder us from just being.

How do objects and people appear once all labels are removed? Do you notice any bits of nothing in-between objects?

'There's a wonderful sense of…recognition in that seeing of the something and the nothing together,' as Tony Parsons says in the film, *Who's Driving the Dreambus?*

CHAPTER 8

OTHER CONSIDERATIONS

8.1 Organisation

Some people may wish to organise thoughts by using a journal. It can be rewarding to see the progress you have made from all the earlier entries to when you have reached better ground. Writing in a journal is a form of therapy, and may help you to feel you have 'got things off your chest,' particularly if you are going through a difficult time.

Declutter, tidy and clean when you can to enhance your environment and generate confidence in doing something productive. A chaotic environment can translate to mind, adding unnecessary stress.

As Robert Satterfield says in *Anxiety*, 'Just pick one drawer or shelf in your home to organise each day. This will make it not as overwhelming.'

Anxiety has been known to make a hoarder out of a person. Satterfield goes on to explain that 'This is because they are afraid to throw (an item) out because they fear they might need it in the future.'

Bear this in mind and ask yourself: *do I really need this item?*

8.2 Blocks

Sometimes we create anxious 'blocks' for ourselves about what we can and cannot do, and about how events will or will not pan out in the future. These become troublesome. It is like we create these blocks to protect us from the future, to give leeway for events going wrong before they actually do. Vernon Howard says in *How to Overcome Fear & Anxiety*, 'Having identified ourselves with the (anxious) thoughts…(then) as long as I'm afraid I feel OK…I'm afraid to come to the end of my fear…the death of fear would of course be the end of me.'

What happens once we learn to trust in the unknown? What happens when we know in as full a way as possible the fact that the future is totally unknown? If we cannot know what the future holds, what can we do?

For a start we can do what we can in the present moment, step by step, and have trust and therefore confidence in that things will work out. Even if they do not or they take a curveball to what we were expecting, the fact that we learned to have that trust gave us confidence at that time, which in turn has given us a tool we can re-use in future. The tool is more confidence via learned experience if events do not turn out the way we expect next time.

8.3 Decision-Making

Decision-making cuts down anxiety. You do not have all those worries swirling around in your head when you have made clear, reasoned decisions. Once you have made them, be at peace with them. In his book, *How to Stop Worrying and Start Living*, Dale Carnegie claims that he banishes about 90% of his worries 'by taking these four steps:

1. Writing down precisely what I am worrying about.

2. Writing down what I can do about it.

3. Deciding what to do.

4. Starting immediately to carry out that decision.'

I will corrupt this model slightly to fit in with how I would think about this and to keep in line with the principles shared in this book:

Make a considered reasoning of why you are worrying, of what you worrying about and whether you believe this worry, and then make a considered decision about what you are going to do about it.

Choose the model that works best, or take the parts of the model(s) that work best for you. I think starting immediately to carry out the decision is a wise idea by Carnegie as it cuts down procrastination and gets the ball rolling right away. The only caveat I would make here is that you may not be feeling up to making a decision yet, or potentially will want to let the situation 'breathe' some more before making a decision.

If you are unsure about these models and are still having trouble making a decision, then try breaking down the decision at hand into manageable chunks of smaller decisions, in a similar way to the tool used in the subchapter, 'One Small Step;' starting off with one little task.

8.4 Helping Others

Robert Satterfield also mentions random acts of kindness. These will not only help someone else feel good but will also make **you** feel good, increasing your confidence. I would also add that volunteering has proved to be very helpful for me.

It is tough in our busy lives especially if we have full-time jobs to find time for volunteering. However, if we are able to find the time, then it is a great way of boosting your confidence at the same time as knowing that you are helping others. In a one-on-one situation with a person that you are helping, it will help both you and the other person, and if you can manage volunteering in a team environment then you will meet some great like-minded people who also want to help, perhaps making a friend or two along the way. It could do wonders for your confidence especially if you have social anxiety.

8.5 Exercise

Exercise is one of those words that evokes joy for some and dread for others. The good news for the latter is that positive effects need only little effort, relatively speaking. On www.medium.com, this is explained: 'Even small amounts of exercise have been shown to improve mood, so a simple 10 minute walk may help to relax frayed nerves. Then there are specific exercises that are often used for relaxation, such as yoga, Tai chi and Qi-gong...generally studies have found these exercises can reduce anxiety and depression.'

Exercise relaxes muscles, and it releases endorphins and adrenalin. A fact less well-known is that it also releases serotonin and dopamine as detailed on www.verywellmind.com.

8.6 Foods

On www.psycom.net there is a list of foods that help with anxiety. Some of these are blueberries, almonds, kale, yoghurt and asparagus. This website suggests using asparagus spears as a replacement for fries.

Good heavens. What will they think of next?

8.7 Herbs

Chris Kilham is an interesting chap. There are videos of him online talking about herbs that can help with anxiety, and these can be found on YouTube. Some herbs that can help are: schizandra, ashwagandha, passion flower, rhodiola rosea, hops, lavender, skullcap, kava, St John's wort, chamomile, valerian and lemon balm. Unfortunately, with many of these, not enough research has been done to determine whether these herbs are positively effective or if they are completely safe. In a lot of cases, research has led to contradictory results and statements from different organisations. For example, according to www.sciencedirect.com passion flower has been shown to be genotoxic to mice, yet it is also generally recognized as safe (GRAS) for use in foods in the USA according to www.accessdata.fda.gov.

Be sure to look up information and/or to check with your doctor before taking anything you are unsure of. Find out whether a herb has disagreeable drug interactions with any medications you might be taking. For example, St John's wort should **not** be used in conjunction with antidepressant medications as it can raise serotonin to unsafe levels.

8.8 Laughter

In the words of Robert Satterfield, 'Smiling releases endorphins, serotonin…(and) there are so many health benefits from lowering blood pressure to boosting the immune system that it is worth taking laughter seriously.' He goes on to say that 'Ten minutes of laughter can actually reduce stress by up to 70%.'

Why not try watching a comedy you like when you feel anxious? It is also a great way to distract yourself if you are struggling with intense anxiety-based bodily symptoms.

There are other sources too that indicate positive results from laughter such as on www.royalsociety publishing.org: 'A study by Oxford University found that pain thresholds become "significantly higher" after laughter…and saw this as being due to laughter itself, rather than the mood of the subject. The study suggested that laughter produced an "endorphin-mediated opiate effect." '

Another source from https://www.ncbi.nlm.nih .gov_says the following: 'A handful of small-scale scientific studies have indicated that Laughter Yoga may potentially have some medically beneficial effects, including benefits to cardiovascular health and mood.'

8.9 Sleep

It is healthy for adults to sleep for at least seven hours. Cutting corners with sleep does not bode well for us worriers. According to www.psychcentral.com, 'Neuroscientists have found that sleep deprivation fires up areas of the brain associated with emotional processing. The resulting pattern mimics the abnormal neural activity seen in anxiety disorders.

'Researchers also believe that chronic worriers…are acutely vulnerable to the impact of insufficient sleep.'

8.10 Caffeine Reduction

(Source: www.medium.com) 'Research has shown that too much caffeine can trigger panic or anxiety attacks, especially if you have an anxiety disorder…if you are adding sugar to your coffee this might be adding to the problem as sugar acts as an adrenal stimulant.'

Robert Satterfield in *Anxiety*, comments on how, 'Caffeine is a stimulant that basically causes your body to release adrenaline. Adrenaline is the main cause of panic attacks.'

8.11 Alternative Therapies/Medicines

In the following list are some alternative therapies that can assist with anxiety: reflexology, emotional freedom techniques (EFT), music therapy, art therapy, chiropractic, osteopathy, use of traditional medicine, herbalism, hydrotherapy, reiki, spiritual/faith healing, energy healing, crystal healing, gong resonance, use of a Himalayan salt lamp, hypnotherapy, aromatherapy (including essential oils & bath salts), shiatsu, acupuncture, shamanism, and osteopathy. Of course there are many more and I have tried some of these. Up next I will say which ones I have tried that have worked best for me.

My first acupuncture session was very powerful in a positive way, but future sessions did not have as strong an effect. Reiki for me was the most consistently positive one that I encountered. I have heard that there are other, more powerful energy healing methods but I have not tried them. When I went on antidepressants, it was suggested by my reiki healer that I stop reiki.

Be sure to check with alternative health practitioners and your doctor about safety concerns, drug interactions and contraindications.

It should be pointed out that what has worked for me or for someone else does not necessarily mean it will be the same for you, and indeed therapies and medicines that have not worked so well for me or someone else may work wonders for you.

8.12 The Traditional Route

The importance of seeing a General Practitioner (GP) for anxiety cannot be underestimated. Do not be afraid to get a second opinion from another doctor if you are left unsatisfied by one as some doctors will have more advanced knowledge and interest in mental health than others. Doctors may suggest medication such as antidepressants or give you the choice of being referred to staff involved in community programmes, cognitive behavioural therapy (CBT), acceptance and commit-ment therapy (ACT), counselling, and so forth. Forming a bond or trust with a particular GP that you feel comfortable with will likely make the entire process easier.

CHAPTER 9

FIGHT OR FLIGHT?

The situation: we are stuck in a room we really do not want to be in. About to take place is something that will trigger our anxiety. It is public speaking or suchlike. If we are very anxious, the fight or flight reaction is bound to be kicking in. One on hand, we will want to get away from the room but we know that if we can manage and even love our fear, then we do not need to get away from it. We will, in all likelihood, feel embarrassed should we escape the room which will not help our cycle of fear. I use the word *cycle* because we can temporarily alleviate escalation by leaving the room, but we will still have the same problem with fear if we re-enter it or if we face a similar situation in the future. Of course, if you really feel you need to get away and are too shaken to feel you can manage your fear, then by all means leave the room. But if we feel able to manage our fear, then it is helpful to remember we are there because we want to be there, in one way or another, even if our reasoning is purely monetarily based or as a means to an end. In most cases, if given the fight or flight option, we will stay and fight. But if we 'fight' through it, we are likely to feel very uncomfortable and wish it to be over, maybe feeling embarrassed at how nervous we are. **The more you fight anxiety, the more it wins**.

That is why the fight or flight analogy is not a concept to overthink if there is the wish to manage fear. When the time feels right for us, we can at some level look fear in the face and say, *Hi fear, how are you doing? I can see you. You are not that big and scary. Let's have a cup of tea and be friends.*

Perhaps loving your fear already feels better than fighting it?

Dr. John P. Forsyth, in considering anxiety says, 'If it (your anxiety) were a tiny child placed in your arms...or a butterfly in your hands—would you squash it and throw it away or would you gently hold it and maybe bring it close?'

Particularly at times of difficulty such as public speaking, we conceivably experience negative thoughts such as, *I can't do this*, or *why can't I be more confident like other people*, or *I feel useless*.

It is easy then to have the tendency to tell our negative thoughts to shut up or leave us alone. This is an example of us fighting. We are susceptible to losing against negative thoughts the more we fight them because negative thoughts are not going to disappear. If you tell one negative thought to shut up, it is only going to re-arise when it feels like it. And then what about all the other negative thoughts that could rise and re-arise? We are back in the cycle of fear.

As Dr. John P. Forsyth says, 'Something we've learned from a very young age (is) that control works so well outside of us…if you don't like the colours of the walls in your bedroom, you can go and buy some paint and change them—there's so many places outside of our skin where control works wonderfully, and then naturally we learn that it must work well for our thoughts and our feelings especially (with) things we don't like very much, so as we experience those, we tend to want to control them and get rid of them and change them…science shows that actually makes things worse.'

If we remember how important concentration is to setting us free, in a way that is relaxed and does not feel like we are overly trying, then how could we apply this for watching our thoughts? What happens if we just watch a thought? What if we watch it as though we are in a safe place watching passing traffic? What happens if, whilst we are watching it, we decide not to judge, good or bad, accepting it is just a thought, knowing it will pass.

To use the traffic analogy, it may occur to you to make the vehicle more interesting the more interesting the thought, such as: *Here comes a wacky thought, it is like a spaceship passing by.* Have fun with it why not. Although this is not in keeping with traditional mindfulness, the point of the exercise is, to once again, find the method that works best for you, that you can use and re-use whenever you like. If you get bored of looking at the thought(s) then turn your attention to mindfully, and without judgment, look at what it feels like to be bored. Have that childlike wonder we mentioned before to watch your boredom. Quite the paradox you might say.

There goes another thought, that is interesting, you might say. Befriend your thoughts even if they are not the thoughts you want to hear.

Look at your mind, look at it go. Look at all those many racing thoughts. Look how powerful and amazing your mind is.

Everyone has anxiety. We have anxiety just a bit more than some other people. That is just who we are.

As Dr. John P. Forsyth says, 'Anxiety isn't a choice.'

What happens if we are able to accept that we have anxiety a bit more, maybe a lot more than some people? That is just us. That's OK. Perfectly OK. What makes us unique after all? You are perfectly imperfect. You are OK.

If your voice drops and you do not speak as confidently as you would like, particularly in the middle of a situation you may find anxious like public speaking for example, then there is no need to fight it. There is no need to be annoyed at yourself. Watch it. Make space for it. How does it feel to have the unconfident voice? Objectively, without judgment, just watch it. Does the next thing you want to say flow better? Maybe you can say it a bit more confidently now.

Let us explore, in these situations, how we piss ourselves off with our thoughts: *oh God, why does it have to start on such a bad footing? Why's it always me? Why can't I speak more confidently? Why can he do it? Why can she do it? I forgot what I was going to say now, my mind's a blank.*

It feels appropriate at this juncture to take a look at the Buddha's parable of the second arrow. If, for example, we trip on a stone as we are walking—see this as the 'first arrow.' In other words, that's life. The first arrow is just what happens in life and we can observe it nonjudgmentally as nothing more than that. If we then look for fault and blame, and think things like, *why can't I pay more attention to where I am walking? I've made such a fool of myself and now everyone is looking at me. Everyone else can walk normally, why can't I?* All these thoughts represent the second arrow, or the third, fourth and so on. All the arrows after the first are what we shoot at ourselves. The more arrows we shoot, the more we are going to hurt.

Let us now move on to observing our resistance in a situation. We can think different thoughts that help us, depending on the right thought for the right situation.

How do we know what the right thought for a situation is?

This is something we develop over time, with trial and error, and with wisdom. We develop a more apt sense of which thoughts match with the right situation **and** whether to stay with them or let them go. We may even elect to say such thoughts out loud if we prefer. Just make sure no-one else is around, or they might think you are talking to them. When it feels right, in a certain situation, we can think, *no resistance.* Think it more than once if it feels right to you. You may feel a lessening of bodily tension. You may feel nothing. It doesn't matter. Watch without judgment. Try thinking to yourself: *I'm not resisting anything. I'm not resisting one inch of what is going on for me at the moment, even if it is uncomfortable.* You could try thinking: *I'm not even trying.* How good does it feel not to try?

You can achieve brilliantly peaceful states in meditation and mindfulness without feeling a sense of trying. Presence can be can be transported to any situation because you are not actually trying to do anything when you are meditating or being mindful. You are not **doing** anything, you are simply **being**.

Rather than saying something like, *you just need to be*, which a lot of people say or variations thereof, sometimes to get in that 'being state,' you need to remember those other little thoughts first sometimes to help you on your way like: *no trying; no resistance.* You may of course at this moment decide that what feels like the best option is to try and love your fear. To love that anxious thought.

Whether you observe and nonjudgmentally watch, whether you do not try, whether you do not resist, or whether you actively try and befriend your thought, choose what you feel works best in a given situation. How could you put your own 'stamp' or twist on any of these thoughts to suit you? Are there any entirely new original thoughts that work for you in this moment unrelated to the previous examples? No situation in life is exactly the same and no-one else's experience of the world is quite like yours. Repeat the techniques that work for you but be aware that too much repetition of what worked before can dull the mind. What you are doing or saying or thinking now—the profundity of the message you want to say to your brain may feel as though it becomes dimmed over time and with repetition. You are saying to your brain there is an important message here that will help me, but the brain is bored and seeks new stimuli. You say the words but you do not feel them. Well, not in the same way anymore. At this point you search for the next technique that will work for the moment as it is now. The technique is like a volcano. The technique that worked before is feasibly dormant in power rather than extinct. So lay off that technique for a while and let it cool off. See if it feels right at a later time, space, place, and whether it still holds power for you then.

When advancing and becoming more deeply involved with our methods of meditation and mindfulness—in this case with the intention of managing and loving our fear—it is easy to get ahead of ourselves as we learn new techniques and forget what worked before. Never forget what worked before. Never lose track of the power of simplicity. All of this information I am saying may seem like a complex networked web. But I am giving you lots of different techniques to be used simply. To corrupt a Gil Fronsdal phrase, *if it's not simple, it's not mindful.*

Indeed, we can see simplicity more clearly as we become more involved and erudite in our practice of meditation and mindfulness. An advanced meditative technique—that is best to use as we go deeper and become very still in our practice—is if we think to ourselves, *don't concentrate on anything.*

If it suits you, you could adapt this phrase to: *don't think about anything,* or simply, *don't think,* or *don't concentrate.*

Here we are met with another paradox. By thinking these thoughts, we can feel our concentration getting stronger. We notice the power of simplicity and how the power of simplicity can aid us. We can feel an easement of our senses and a letting go of what we feel we 'should' be concentrating on or trying to 'do.' That is to say, a letting go of trying altogether.

9.1 Technique Usage & Meditation

All of the techniques previously mentioned can be delved into mindfully throughout the day, or during meditation when there is a quiet moment; even in bed. But be aware that if we meditate then it is better to try sitting up in a chair feeling relaxed with an almost straight posture, back arched very slightly, with a cushion for lower back support if necessary, and your head not slumped downwards, nor lifted upward of central. Eyes closed or half-closed. Feet perpendicular to each other. If you can, then try the lotus or half lotus method for sitting on the floor. If you are not sure what these are then according to B. K. S. Iyengar in *Light on Yoga*, 'From sitting cross-legged on the floor...one foot is placed on top of the opposite thigh with its sole facing upward and heel close to the abdomen. The other foot is then placed on the opposite thigh as symmetrically as possible.' Try and have your knees touching the ground.

(Source: Swami Satyananda Saraswati, Asana Pranayama Mudra Bandha) 'In half lotus...one leg is bent and resting on the floor, the other leg is bent with the foot in lotus position. It is an easier meditation position than full lotus.'

These positions—whether on the floor or sitting in a chair—are better than lying down as it is easier to concentrate and you are less likely to fall asleep. But equally it is a lovely way to fall asleep at night if that is your aim.

Standing up straight is also a good way to meditate and if you do this then do not worry about falling over in a deep meditation as this is extremely unlikely. Gil Fronsdal said that in over twenty years of teaching he has only on one occasion seen someone fall over whilst meditating standing up.

Mix it up, see what you like. What I know is that many of these methods have been very successful for me. I hope they can be successful for you too.

CHAPTER 10

WHEN FEELING BAD

'It's natural to turn away from pain…and the problem is when we turn it on ourselves and we start to try to get away from ourselves—our own internal pain, our own feelings, our bodily sensations—and that sets us up for struggle.'

- Dr. John P. Forsyth

The reason I have put, 'When Feeling Bad,' rather than, 'If Feeling Bad' as the title of this chapter is because there are definitely times when we will feel bad. To shy away from this would not be compatible with successful resolution. One of the messages of this book is acceptance. Just like accepting our fear, accepting when we feel bad is an important first step in managing it. Accepting yourself is the first step to loving yourself.

How we manage when we feel bad can be one of the hardest things to do. I am still working on it on a weekly basis. But I have learnt a lot over the years and hopefully you can find some useful tidbits to take away from my experiences. If you are a bit of a perfectionist like me and have a strong work ethic and like to get things done rather than watching others do them, then

I think coping whilst feeling bad can be even harder to achieve. But it is possible. A psychotherapist once said to me that perfectionists run out of money or time.

10.1 Tiredness

Anxiety is often tiring. It can be even more tiring if, for example, you are an introvert anxious about dealing with lots of people, and then you have to deal with lots of people in a day.

That is why pacing is important, and one reason why I have put this sentence on a new paragraph. As a bit of a war geek, I see pacing as a bit like rationing food during wartime. It is hard to get excited about rationing as it is not very fun, but we know it makes sense to conserve energy. We know that if we race around doing all the different things we need to do, then by the end of the day we are going to be very tired and not feel like doing anything for the evening when perhaps we would like to be productive. This can then lead to frustration, feeling so tired and yet bedtime is so far away. At this point it is natural to try and remedy the situation by watching crap TV.

If there is a physical illness or pain or mobility issue when already suffering from problems with anxiety, perhaps in conjunction with anxiety's good friend, depression, too, then the physical problems really can compound and amplify our mental health problems. Suddenly physical problems that seemed not so big a deal—maybe before a specific mental health problem— like having a bad foot or head cold can become far greater problems. Of course, people with one mental health problem often have another mental health problem that may be dissimilar. In only the sphere of anxiety, they might have two or three different problems or disorders. So if there is more than one physical problem as well as more than one mental health problem, then it can be hard for others to really understand what we are going through.

If we think once again about wisdom, with trial and error and experience, we learn more honestly what we can and cannot do in a day, and the extent to which we can do them. It makes sense to do a bit at a time throughout the day and evening if we want to have as fully productive as possible a twenty-four hours.

If anxiety makes me tired, can I try and cut off anxiety?

Well, try battling it if that works better for you. I have found an example that supports this theory, with thanks to Robert Satterfield: 'In times of stress, our brains are wired to create self-talk that can increase our feelings of fear. (Soldiers) are experienced to fight against inner self-talk and focus on positive portions of experiences. With practice they're easily able to ignore or even erase the negativity.'

In my experience, and as such, the message throughout this book is that: battling will more likely make us tired because we will become angry and frustrated at our anxiety, which will add to our cycle of tiredness. Therefore, I believe that at least a level of acceptance is once again required. You might feel bad right now but it won't always be like this.

In such situations, as awful as you may feel inside, it is good to remember how you can say to yourself: *OK, time to check in with myself. I am having a bad day but it is just temporary. If I look at the bigger picture, tomorrow is a new day and each new dawn on the horizon offers new hope.*

Sometimes we have to look beyond our current situation to find the logic and reasoning to help our current situation.

But the pain feels like it is always going to be there. How do you know that I will not have this problem forever?

What I mean when I say, 'It won't always be like this' is based on how we perceive the problem. We cannot always change how we physically feel but we **can** choose how we relate to it.

Look at the example of Thích Quàng Đức, the Buddhist monk who burned himself alive for political protest. He burned without flinching in deep meditation. Now obviously this is an extreme example and I would never endorse self-harm or suicide. However, the example does show how we can use the power of our minds even in cases of extreme physical anguish. The Buddha himself—after it was said that he became enlightened—at the age of eighty, had a bad back, but it did not bother him because he had already lost attachment to his body.

10.2 Telling Others

Unfortunately, there are some people who do not really understand people who have mental health problems. Even though the person with the problem may be really struggling underneath the surface, they may appear 'OK' on the surface. That person on the surface, or in actuality, might not be doing too badly that particular day. The thing about mental health problems is that they can fluctuate so much that you can feel not as bad one minute and then the next minute or the next day you are in a totally different place. So having mental health problems is often a very up and down journey.

A lot of us hide these problems from others, so even when we are not feeling great, we will still make an effort to hide the problems because we are worried the other person might not understand. We might feel the need to do what we think is 'acting tough' by not talking about problems in polite society. In the environment we were brought up in or during our experience at school, it could be that it felt impossible to talk about these problems.

Stigmas and attitudes are changing, and ten or twenty years ago health professionals could say things to you that they would not be able to nowadays. Twelve years ago I went to a doctor about social anxiety. When I was explaining to him how much I was struggling with this problem, he looked at me, shrugged his shoulders and said, 'What problem?' His palms faced the sky to emphasise his question. Because I was able to articulate to him the problem confidently, he failed to understand why I had a problem as he could not see my social anxiety. But I did not usually have this problem in one-on-one conversations. I had a different kind of social anxiety that manifested when with groups of people rather than with one person at a time.

In time before my example, I heard of a case when someone went to a university counsellor with depression. The counsellor told them something to the effect of, 'You just have to get on with it.'

Hopefully health professionals are more clued up on mental health these days. Yes, we still have a long way to go, but mental health is in the public eye more often now and one can only hope that it is becoming easier to talk about and easier to understand. There is the realisation too that one in three people will get a mental health problem in their lifetime.

Because of the way stigma still exists about mental health, because we are sometimes worried about how we are perceived by others, because of how we have been brought up, because of attitudes of the past and because of our environment, we can view mental disorders such as anxiety as a weakness which then leads us to feel shame.

What if we were to start thinking about our anxiety as we would if unfortunately, we had lost a leg, accepting it for the rest of our days. Purely in that way they are no different, but we also have to acknowledge the fact that someone who loses a leg would be a lot more noticeable to others because people respond to physical problems more than mental problems, for the most part because they can see them.

Yet what we experience in our inner world is just as important as the problems that people can see. What if we were to break down any social constructs, stigmas or views and sayings of others, and instead just see circumstances as they actually are: I have more anxiety than most people; I have one leg less than most people.

That is what they are inherently. Anything added on top of that is conceptual, whether it be from others or what we add ourselves. This is why we have no need to feel ashamed, and also why it is important to tell others when we have these mental health problems. As others cannot see them and may well assume that everything is going well with you, underneath the surface we could dying to say to someone, *can't you see how I feel?*

10.3 Escapism

It may seem contradictory to previous messages, and nothing in life is black and white, but we all like to escape from time to time. It is unrealistic, particularly if we are not far along in treating our anxiety, to expect to be continually mindful or to regularly meditate. Such is the nature of anxiety and mental health problems that we are going to have off days where we do not feel up to managing our anxiety in this way.

It is nice to take a break. You might not feel ready to manage your problems through meditation or mindfulness. Many people with mental health problems like to play video games as a form of escapism. Be careful about escaping with drink and drugs because they can exacerbate the mental health problem(s). Funnily enough, it is during the periods when we are particularly affected by our mental health problems, that if we stick at it, we can experience some of the most powerful insights during our meditations, mindfulness, and our art if we are artistically minded— art being another terrific method of therapy and/or escapism.

CHAPTER 11

CRISIS

I have used *crisis* as a broad term to include any form of extreme anxiety including panic. In such instances, please take suitable medical advice. I have had quite a lot of experiences of extreme anxiety and panic. This chapter will cover what has helped me in such circumstances.

Distraction is an important technique to use when encountering extreme anxiety. I have found this especially true the more active I am. Productive manual tasks that 'take you outside of yourself,' such as loading a dishwasher, doing some washing up and cleaning. Perhaps some relaxing music can be playing in the background. Doing creates confidence. There is a sense of accomplishment from these tasks and your confidence grows during the task and after completion.

In a crisis, you are too het up sometimes to do your usual calming techniques like deep breathing or sometimes the more you do them, the more they seem to get you worked up because it is hard to relax. There is a subconscious anxiety in knowing that you are really trying to control your manifest anxiety. You are desperate to heal yourself. Have confidence that with time your body will naturally calm down if you are focussing on confidence-building tasks away from the self that is too anxious to calm.

Distraction can be done on your own or with someone else, whichever works for you best. If you want someone to help you then it is best if you can find someone you know you can rely on to be a calming influence rather than someone who, although has good intentions, might not be the most calming to have around you at such a time.

I will never forget when I was in a crisis one time. You may call it a mild panic attack or an extended period of extreme anxiety as I prefer to call it. Anyway, I was shaking and I just could not relax. I ended up calling a panic helpline. I cannot remember if I called two different numbers or whether I was passed from one different person to the next but I had two conversations with two different helpers, and I was struck by something, in a way I did not think I would be.

The first person I spoke to you was very nice and very caring. I could really hear her concern for me and she was telling me that I was not thinking straight and that I was slurring my words. She said I needed to get to a GP as soon as I could. I really appreciated her concern and how she clearly cared. Unfortunately, I felt more anxious after speaking to her because the fact that she sounded so concerned made me believe I had more reason than I realised to be anxious about my anxiety.

An important point to remember is—and I think people have trouble understanding this if they do not suffer such crises themselves—that it is very hard to be rational at these times and think logically. Also it is difficult for your body to subconsciously think in a logival way, if you like, if you can conceive a body as thinking, but it is hard for your body to act rationally because it is so worked up, so everything becomes very instinctual: someone else sounds anxious = your body tightens and you become more anxious.

Even if you know really that they are just trying to help you and they want to show you that they care, your body becomes more anxious even if you can rationalise the situation with your mind. Therefore, if you are acting as the 'helper,' then it is important to be very sensitive and select in the words you choose to say to the person going through a crisis. Often less is more.

What then really struck me was the next call. When I spoke to the next woman I was at first a bit surprised and angry about her manner. I started speaking to her telling her I thought I was having a panic attack or something of that nature, and she could obviously hear the extreme anxiety in my voice, and it felt like she almost dismissed what I had said. She replied saying something like, 'Oh, OK,' in a very matter-of-fact way, as if everything was perfectly normal, and then she asked me something like, 'So what have you been up to today?' It was something very trivial like that, and I remember thinking: *can you not hear how anxious I am?! Help me here! You need to help me, I'm in a desperate situation.*

She knew that, of course, and she was using a distraction technique, I would estimate, to normalise my state, to make me think of more normal things like what I did today to take me out of this anxiety bubble and focus my attention on something else. I realised this soon enough, but at the start of the conversation I just felt negativity towards her, as if she did not really care for my plight.

By the end of this conversation, I felt calmer than I had done speaking to the previous woman. I learnt a lot from that. It showed me a new way I can act for others who might be going through a similar situation to how I was at that time. This example is an example of the power of distraction. It can be difficult to maintain because you are overwrought and it takes a while for you and your body to calm down.

So have in mind a good dose of distraction, imaginably in different forms to encourage distraction's overall staying power. Playing a game takes a lot of focus and can help when in a crisis, providing that it is probably an easy-going game with no violence etcetera.

Valium, if used sensibly, can be a help in a crisis and I have found sertraline to be good for anxiety. Sertraline is an antidepressant of the SSRI family. For less drastic measures, the Bach flower remedies like Rescue Remedy does something for me and I know of others who have gained something from them too. If you are looking for other natural ways to manage anxiety, then referring back to the 'Herbs' subchapter in the 'Other Considerations' chapter may be of help to you.

In Robert Satterfield's *Anxiety*, it is said that, 'When we think that panic attacks are bad, the feeling of panic is somewhat fuelled…if you acknowledge that something's not inherently bad or good and that it's merely a sensation, then your panic will actually decrease. The sensation may persist, but you will be at peace.'

In regards to our negative thoughts about panic attacks, Satterfield goes on to say that, 'It is extremely difficult to not think about something when you know that you should not think about it. Just know this fact and spare yourself the struggle in the midst of a panic attack.'

Slow, deep breathing will help, as will exercise in a crisis. As mentioned in *Rewire Your Anxious Brain*, it is helpful to 'pace, or exercise during a panic attack. This will burn off the excess adrenaline that's in your system and should help shorten the panic attack.' Remember that 'a panic attack won't physically hurt you…the sensations you're experiencing are signs of a healthy, reactive body,' the book goes on to say.

In the moment of crisis, you could try to be in what Tolle calls 'the stillness.' An extreme acceptance and surrender of what is. Being in the stillness of the moment.

If it is raining outside, do we keep standing outside and get drenched or do we come inside for comfort? In the same way, if our anxiety is pouring down on us, then if we are able to, we must look inside; for distraction will help us and keep us on an even keel for now but will only paper over the cracks in the long run, like a tent for the rain. It is only through looking inside that we can get to the root of the problem and find how to love our fear.

However, if you are having a panic attack or similarly intense kind of crisis, being with the stillness for prolonged periods of time can be very difficult which is why I would personally opt for distraction as the main method, and work on 'the stillness' in less agitated times. If you feel that in a crisis you would rather work on the stillness option, go for it.

I will not go into stillness in this way too much because that would be getting into another book, and Mr. Tolle might sue me. But the idea of it is that no problems can arise when you achieve extremely deep stillness by looking into the self, not looking for a stillness that is something to grab, something to find, but actually to look within because it is already there. From that stillness no problems can arise. When you are truly still—in that stillness there is no identification with ego and you enter a greater intelligence outside of conditioned thinking. However bad the crisis, there can always be a snippet of gratitude to experience. That gratitude can be for anything, but in that stillness, come it will. Gratitude makes one feel better, does it not?

Feel the grass against your toes. Biologically your body has decided to be here; your parents made sure of it. So be here. Can you be here better?

Impermanence is the state of all things, and so it is true in difficult situations of crises as well. As Lao Tzu said, 'A violent wind does not outlast the morning; a squall of rain does not outlast the day.'

Lao Tzu founded Daoism in China in the 6th century BC. Daoism points to a life of simplicity and of living in nature. It predates, and partly influences Buddhism, which in turn has now had a wide-ranging influence on the Western world especially in terms of meditation and mindfulness to help us relax.

A crisis can seem so horrible. It might feel like it is for forever, leaving you unsure if you can stand it much longer. It won't. You can. Hang in there. You have a place in this world, and beyond. You help weave the fabric of the universe.

IF YOU ENJOYED THIS BOOK

&

want to be informed about Joel's latest books then...

Sign up for updates using the link below

&

Get a FREE chapter of Joel's upcoming novel, *Jim & Martha*:
www.joelschueler.com/free

About Joel Schueler

Joel is from London and has a BA(Hons) in English Literature & Creative Writing from the University of Wales, Aberystwyth. His works have been accepted across nine different countries in over thirty publications including Pennsylvania Literary Journal, The Bangalore Review & The Brasilia Review. He is a zealous writer of music, lyrics, comedy & more.

Connect with Joel

Website: www.joelschueler.com

Twitter: www.twitter.com/JoelSchueler?lang=en

Instagram: www.instagram.com/joelschueler_writer

Facebook: www.facebook.com/authorjoelschueler

YouTube: www.youtube.com/channel/UCwrenJpKQXd4sYInXN PbcFA/featured?view_as=subscriber

OTHER BOOKS BY JOEL SCHUELER

Fiction

Jim & Martha: A Novel on Eco Living…COMING SOON

APPENDIX 1:

BIBLIOGRAPHY

Below are listed the references to books used. Thank you to all these authors:

Anxiety: Self Help Guide for Overcoming Anxiety, Phobias, Depression and Panic Attacks for Both Adults and Children Through Meditation and CBT Therapy: Stop Negative Thoughts and Increase Confidence - Robert Satterfield

How to Stop Worrying and Start Living - Dale Carnegie

The Power of Now - Eckhart Tolle

Rewire Your Anxious Brain: How to Use the Neuroscience of Fear to End Anxiety, Panic and Worry - Catherine M Pittman, Elizabeth M Karle

B. K. S. Iyengar (1979). Light on Yoga. Thorsons

Feel the Fear and Do It Anyway – Susan Jeffers

Appendix 2:

Other Resources in Full

Below are listed the other references in full used for this book. Thank you to all those involved with these references:

(Film) Who's Driving the Dreambus? - Boris Jänsch, Claire Jänsch
Swami Satyananda Saraswati *(1996)*. Asana Pranayama Mudra Bandha (PDF*)*. Munger, Bihar, India: Yoga Publications Trust

Laughter yoga & cardiovascular effects
https://www.ncbi.nlm.nih.gov/pubmed/22894892

Laughter; pain thresholds
https://royalsocietypublishing.org/doi/full/10.1098/rspb.2011.1373

How to overcome Anxiety - Dr. Claire Weekes
https://www.youtube.com/watch?v=MHr4a71XGJE&t=2393s

OCD & Anxiety Disorders: Crash Course Psychology #29
https://www.youtube.com/watch?v=aX7jnVXXG5o

Cherokee Proverb
https://krexy.com/native-american-quote

John Cleese: "So, Anyway..." | Talks at Google
https://www.youtube.com/watch?v=2-p44-9S4O0

How to Overcome Fear & Anxiety - Vernon Howard
https://www.youtube.com/watch?v=nD7W6Z5F9xE

MG Craske; MB Stein (24 June 2016). "Anxiety".
Lancet. 388
https://www.thelancet.com/journals/lancet/article/PIIS
0140-6736(16)30381-6/fulltext

Foods for anxiety
https://www.psycom.net/foods-that-help-with-anxiety-
and-stress/

Lotus Position
https://en.wikipedia.org/wiki/Lotus_position

Lao Tzu quote
https://en.wikiquote.org/wiki/Laozi

Sleep loss effects on anxiety
https://psychcentral.com/news/2013/06/27/sleep-loss-
increases-anxiety-especially-among-worriers/56531.html

Fear & anxiety definitions
https://www.verywellmind.com/fear-and-anxiety-
differences-and-similarities-2584399

Exercise

https://www.verywellmind.com/exercise-and-improving-your-mood-2223781

Ways of reducing anxiety
https://medium.com/parkinsons-uk/7-ways-to-reduce-anxiety-research-explained-9ab53a7b04b1

Dr. Karl Albrecht quote
https://www.thecoachingtoolscompany.com/5-types-of-fears-dr-karl-albrecht/

Passion flower
https://en.wikipedia.org/wiki/Passiflora#cite_note-24

Passion flower toxicity
https://www.sciencedirect.com/science/article/pii/S0378874109005972?via%3Dihub

Amber Rae interviewed by Joanna Penn, The Creative Penn
https://www.youtube.com/watch?v=4CDoWAglf88

Passion flower safety
https://www.accessdata.fda.gov/scripts/cdrh/cfdocs/cfcfr/CFRSearch.cfm?fr=172.510

Anxiety and PTSD
https://www.bbrfoundation.org/content/researchers-find-brain-circuit-drives-anxiety

Dr. John P. Forsyth interviewed by Michael Sandler, Inspire Nation Show
https://www.youtube.com/watch?v=ol0LU8JIEmg

List of Organisations, Helplines, Charities & Information related to Anxiety

UK

Dial 999 in an emergency

NHS 111
Call: 111 and you can get help if you have an urgent medical problem and you're not sure what to do.
https://111.nhs.uk/
If you have difficulties communicating or hearing, you can:
call 18001 111 on a textphone
use the NHS 111 British Sign Language (BSL) interpreter service if you're deaf and want to use the phone service
http://www.interpreternow.co.uk/nhs111/

NHS Mental Health Services
https://www.nhs.uk/using-the-nhs/nhs-services/mental-health-services/

NHS Local Mental Health Service search
https://www.nhs.uk/Service-Search/Mental-health-information-and-support/LocationSearch/330#

NHS Local Mental Health Service search for Young People
https://www.nhs.uk/Service-Search/Mental-health-support-for-young-people/LocationSearch/1430

NHS Local Anxiety Services Search
https://www.nhs.uk/Service-Search/Anxiety/LocationSearch/1810

Samaritans
(For anyone in emotional distress or at risk of suicide)
Call free on 116 123 (free 24-hour helpline)
https://www.samaritans.org/

PAPYRUS
(Young suicide prevention society)
0800 068 4141 (Mon to Fri,10am to 5pm & 7 to 10pm. Weekends 2 to 5pm)
www.papyrus-uk.org

No Panic
0844 967 4848 (daily, 10am to 10pm)
(For those who suffer from Panic Attacks, Phobias, Obsessive Compulsive Disorders and other related anxiety disorders including those people who are trying to give up Tranquillizers)
https://www.nopanic.org.uk/

NHS guidelines on How to deal with Panic Attacks
https://www.nhs.uk/conditions/stress-anxiety-depression/coping-with-panic-attacks/

Anxiety Alliance

0845 296 7877 (10-10 daily)
www.anxietyalliance.org.uk

Royal College of Psychiatrists
(Anxiety, Panic and Phobias Page)
https://www.rcpsych.ac.uk/mental-health/problems-
disorders/anxiety-panic-and-phobias

Moodjuice
(For those experiencing troublesome thoughts, feelings
and actions)
https://www.moodjuice.scot.nhs.uk/

Moodjuice Shyness & Social Anxiety Self-Help Guide:
https://www.moodjuice.scot.nhs.uk/shynesssocialphobi
a.asp

CALM
(CALM is the Campaign Against Living Miserably, for
men aged 15 to 35)
0800 58 58 58 (daily, 5pm to midnight)
www.thecalmzone.net

Men's Health Forum
(24/7 stress support for men by text, chat and email)
www.menshealthforum.org.uk

Mental Health Foundation
(Provides information and support for anyone with
mental health problems or learning disabilities)
020 7803 1101
Website: www.mentalhealth.org.uk

OCD Action
(Support for people with OCD)
0845 390 6232 (Mon to Fri, 9.30am to 5pm)
www.ocdaction.org.uk

OCD UK
(Run by people with OCD for people with OCD)
0845 120 3778 (Mon to Fri, 9am to 5pm)
www.ocduk.org

Rethink Mental Illness
(Support and advice for people living with mental illness)
0300 5000 927 (Mon to Fri, 9.30am to 4pm)
www.rethink.org

SANE
(Emotional support, information and guidance for people affected by mental illness, their families and carers)
0300 304 7000 (daily, 4.30 to 10.30pm)
www.sane.org.uk/support
Textcare: comfort and care via text message, sent when the person needs it most:
http://www.sane.org.uk/textcare
Peer support forum: www.sane.org.uk/supportforum

NSPCC
Children's charity dedicated to ending child abuse and child cruelty.
0800 1111 for Childline for children (24-hour helpline)

0808 800 5000 for adults concerned about a child (24-hour helpline)
www.nspcc.org.uk

Refuge
Advice on dealing with domestic violence.
0808 2000 247 (24-hour helpline)
www.refuge.org.uk

Rape Crisis
To find your local services phone: 0808 802 9999
(daily, 12 to 2.30pm, 7 to 9.30pm)
www.rapecrisis.org.uk

Victim Support
0808 168 9111 (24-hour helpline)
www.victimsupport.org

Family Lives
Advice on all aspects of parenting including dealing with bullying.
0808 800 2222 (Mon to Fri, 9am to 9pm. Sat to Sun, 10am to 3pm)
www.familylives.org.uk

Public Speaking Anxiety Helpline
0207 724 6225

Mind
(Mental Health Support)
0300 123 3393 (Mon to Fri, 9am to 6pm)
https://www.mind.org.uk/

Elefriends
(Community Support from Mind)
https://www.elefriends.org.uk/

Together
(Mental Health Support)
020 7780 7300
http://www.together-uk.org/

The Centre for Mental Health
020 7827 8300
https://www.centreformentalhealth.org.uk/

BACP Find a Therapist Directory
(Counselling Services in Your Area)
01455 883300
https://www.bacp.co.uk/search/Therapists

Citizens Advice
https://www.citizensadvice.org.uk/

YoungMinds
(Support for Young People)
020 7336 8445
https://youngminds.org.uk/
Parents' helpline: 0808 802 5544 (Mon to Fri, 9.30am
to 4pm)

Childline
(Support for Children)
0800 1111
https://www.childline.org.uk/

Nightline
(Support for Students by Students)
https://www.nightline.ac.uk/

Age UK
(Support for Senior Citizens)
0800 009966
https://www.ageuk.org.uk/

Lesbian and Gay Switchboard
020 7837 7324
https://switchboard.lgbt/

Time to Change
(Anti-Mental Health Discrimination)
https://www.time-to-change.org.uk

Mental Health Mates
https://mentalhealthmates.co.uk/

PTSD Buddies
https://www.ptsdbuddies.org/

Meetup
(Useful for finding local people and events, including
for mental health)
https://www.meetup.com/

Facebook
(Useful for finding people in groups akin to your
interests, including for mental health)
https://www.facebook.com/

Guideposts Trust
(Mental Health Services)
http://guideposts.org.uk/contact-us/

Relate
(Relationship Support)
0300 100 1234
https://www.relate.org.uk/

Education Support Partnership
(Support for Teachers)
08000 562 561
https://www.educationsupportpartnership.org.uk/

Carers UK
(Support for Carers)
https://www.carersuk.org/Home

Anxiety UK
(Mental Health Support)
08444 775 774
https://www.anxietyuk.org.uk/

For Dental Anxiety Email Support:
dentalanxiety@anxietyuk.org.uk

Worldwide

List of Worldwide Mental Health Hotlines
http://www.cocoonais.com/mental-health-hotlines-worldwide/

Mental Health Support for Gamers
www.checkpointorg.com

List of World Suicide Crisis Lines
https://en.wikipedia.org/wiki/List_of_suicide_crisis_lin
es

Psycom
(Mental Health general information and self-
assessment)
www.psycom.net

International Association for Suicide Prevention (IASP)
https://www.iasp.info/resources/Crisis_Centres/

International Suicide Hotlines
http://www.suicide.org/international-suicide-
hotlines.html

Your Life Counts
(Global list of Crisis Lines searchable by location)
https://yourlifecounts.org/find-help/

Befrienders Worldwide
https://www.befrienders.org/

Online Live Chat for Suicide Prevention:
https://www.7cups.com/
https://www.imalive.org/

46557309R00066

Printed in Poland
by Amazon Fulfillment
Poland Sp. z o.o., Wrocław